# Kindle

By
Paulann Petersen

△△△△△△△△△

MOUNTAINS
& RIVERS
〜〜〜〜〜〜
PRESS

Some of these poems first appeared in *The Alembic*; *By Line*; *Calapooya*; *Fabrication* (26 Books); *Fireweed*; *Manzanita Quarterly*; *The Oregonian*; *Poetry Northwest*; *Take Out*; *West Wind Review*; *Windfall*; and *Yes, Poetry*.

With gratitude to the poets in the Pearls, Odd Mondays, and Poetry Church groups for their responses to earlier versions of some of these poems.

With gratitude to Ce Rosenow, whose remarkable vision and dedication shaped this book.


Book Design: Peace Rose Graphics
Cover Design: Stephen Leflar
Printing: Lithtex Printing, Hillsboro, Oregon
Editorial Assistance: Pui Yin Chiu and Kalah McCaffrey


Mountains and Rivers Press
mountainsandriverspress.org


First Editon

*Kindle* © 2008 Paulann Petersen
ISBN: 0-9793204-1-0
Library of Congress Control Number: 2008921034

*for Dorothy Stafford*
*beloved friend*

For Ann,
with all best
wishes,

Paulann
AUGUST 2008

# CONTENTS

## III. EVERYTHING HERE MUST TOUCH

## IV. BROUGHT HERE FROM AFAR

## V. POLAR FLIGHT

# Introduction

From book to book Paulann Petersen's work has been remarkable for its formal variety and emotional range and with *Kindle* that process continues. Throughout the collection there is a steady quest for a place in the universe – where do we stand? – along with an unsentimental recognition of our mortality. The poems range widely from intimate scenes in the poets' backyard to the Agean, to recollections of the past and explorations of art. Among the latter it is good to see an old favorite – rather neglected these days, it seems – Charles Burchfield, that mysteriously lyrical painter. In "Breugel's Babel" you find the poet's characteristically precise language:

> . . . the thick
> viscous of gossip – that natter –
> oozes like a honeyed tongue.

One notices that there is a hint of vicious in "viscous" as well as the edge "honeyed" gives the idea of gossip – 'I'm telling you this for your own good, friend'. A different kind of precision can be seen in "Gather Close":

> Winter. Time for what's
> told only when light
> makes itself scarce.

The last line makes fine use of a conversational idiom derived from the idea of making yourself scarce – 'Beat it, buddy' – as well as the actual fact of winter's lack of light. Many poets attempt to convert everyday speech to the uses of poetry, but Paulann largely succeeds in doing so. There is also the wit of "For Special Emphasis" which looks at italic letters in a clever way. And of course her use of sensuous detail crops up in poem after poem with rain, for example rendered this way in "Sense":

> You can taste
> only the part of rain falling
> nearest your tongue.
>
> Rain is that small . . . .

Rain and water play significant roles throughout these poems with the poet wisely suggesting that an oceanside spot might be the ideal home for us all or, lacking that, what is near at hand, a river. Water of course dovetails with the ideas of change because it is always in flux just as our lives are. As has been said by someone very wise, you never step twice into the same stream. Rain and sea mingle in "Basin" – "raindrops taste sweet/an ocean in its mild disguise." Or from "Slake":

> With the souls of the dead, I stand
> by a river, breathing the underworld's
> cool perfume.

No matter how formidable the artillery of the long poem may be, the still small voice of the lyric remains the central item in the poet's arsenal, and that is clearly the case here. The longest piece in the book, "Polar Flight," is actually a sequence of linked lyrics – which is not to downplay that poem. 'Flight' is ripe with keen observations and lively language. After several questions about where and what we are, the poet comes to a final one:

> What makes
> the skimming, trembled
> airplane shadow below?

Which also echoes another of the themes of the book: the idea of otherness or the double. The witty "Rorshach" demonstrates this, beginning with

> I am, to begin with, two.
> My own mirror, my own doppel-
> ganger, stand-in,
>
> my own understudy.

and continuing with the idea of doubleness until it concludes by zeroing in on the necessary tension which prevents this "duplicity from/tearing me apart."

There are forces in our society which try very hard to put us in a fixed place – as if those directories in malls with arrows that indicate YOU ARE HERE meant that you had better damn well stay there or else – but the poet knows that the self is slippery and doesn't fall easily into any particular slot saying, Hey, wait a minute you may be here but you're also over there or maybe somewhere else entirely. Paulann Petersen says these things but also adds that the place you find yourself is often a transitional one on the way from here to there – at those times when the seasons change or on the bank of a moving stream or flying over the pole. This rich collection will help readers orient themselves in this volatile world while also giving them the pleasure of savoring a deft and vibrant exploration of language.

– Vern Rutsala

# I.
# A COSMOS WAITING

## GROUNDED

Find the North Star in a clear
night sky. Lie down on the grass,
on the one place that sets
Polaris atop the tip of a great
slope-limbed fir tree
growing near your house.

Quiet for long enough, you'll see
heaven spin. Large and small,
fierce or dim, pieces of light
gyre around one sky-bound spot.
A prayerwheel of other suns
whirls from the star-peak of a tree.

## CALENDAR

Each day ends
only a second away
from another. Each with its own
aphorism, daily dose
of wisdom and regret. One square
in a checkerboard of others,
it takes on its own label,
a number. Maybe it's a big someone's
birthday. Or a small someone,
like the rest of us. Maybe it's a day
uncommon enough for opening a carton
of decorations in the basement.
That number dresses itself
in a red cloak. Then it's gone too.

What smidgen of hours
boxed off on a kitchen wall
wouldn't fly by?—a day
here and overtaken
by its never taken-for-identical
twin coming next.

## AS FALL DAYS CONTINUE
## THEIR ONWARD COUNT

I wrap myself in a garment of summer
that carries me back
to the huge garden plot
I tended for years, then left behind
years ago. Far away,

three hundred miles south
and east of here, I carry
a hoe into rows of sweet corn—
chopping at chickweed, purslane, quackgrass,
at sprouts of plantain. By hand I pull out

the interlopers hiding against
inch-thick stalks, then take a rake
to the path of soft dirt
between each row. Rake and step,
rake and step. But not

heedful enough. I have walked
on the earth I so carefully smoothed.
The corn is in tassel. Pollen drifts, thick—
yellow filling each footprint.
Who knows what grows there now.

# TIME-TRAVEL

The last time I see the man
I was wife to for twenty years
(give or take a year/ give, be taken)
he's fallen asleep while

I sleep, dreaming his face
resting against the steering wheel
of the car he drives. His passenger—
what else?—I cry out, rile him

to open his eyes. My left hand
(ringed? I don't see) reaches over
to turn the wheel a little,
and we're safe. I rouse

from the dream before a blow
of his anger *What the hell?*
*Why didn't you do something*
*sooner?* can travel the distance

between us—the righted car gone,
the road now a part of itself
that lay ahead, out of sight.
I walk it alone, awake.

## SUTURE

The sun rocks back
on its heels, making lower arcs
each day, moving toward
long nights. Summer's flush
slowly leaches out.

I sit in a garden corner. A spider
spins its line from branch to post,
hemming me in. *Sutra,* it gleams—
the sun low enough to make
the strand a thread of light.

I can stay put. I can put
one hand out, moving it in loops
so the spider-weave wraps my skin
in shining coils. Old remedy
stemming a flow of blood.

# A LITTLE PERSPECTIVE

Seen close enough,
tungsten atoms make
a starburst. Farthest galaxies,
a prick of light.

Tungsten traces lay inside
the tomato I ate this morning.
Its globe held in one hand,
I took it into me

bite by bite. Juice and seed
smeared my chin.
*Love apple.*
Small, red sun.

Our galaxy lies inside
a cosmos waiting
to swallow me whole.
Night coming—fast.

## PHANTOM BODY

Above faraway lands, the new moon
floats an upturned curl
on the sky. There, the moon
sprouts prongs, left and right—
becomes a pair of horns
hooking stars. You ask,
*Then where is the bull's body,*
*its gristle and rippling bulk?*
*The paw and shudder?*
*That member big enough*
*to be called just that?*
*Where is semen's milky shine?*

Learn another tongue.
Ask the night.

## RORSCHACH

I am, to begin with, two.
My own mirror, my own doppel-
ganger, stand-in,

my own understudy. I am
the overstatement
of echo, of counter

part and point, each black
smudge the same-egg twin
Siamesed to its mate.

In each direction, a
duplicate. Only my axis mundi
is a sole, a pole of true

north and true south
holding my duplicity from
tearing me in two.

Dear Soul,

A lie I tell sends you out
to range in my extremities.
Uneasy, you roam
my ankles and shins, bumping
inside my feet. I stumble on each
uneven floor.

A generous word I say
calls you back to my core. Steady,
your presence marks the beat sending
blood out to feed me.

Talk to me again. Speak
when we're easiest, in the night.
Promise, and I promise
to listen, harboring close.
I'll name what you say
*gladness,* call it *dream I seek*
and when I wake repeat it
to myself, best as I can.

Yours,
in the sweet of sleep.

# CARRIED FROM THE CURRENT

My house near the Willamette
is only blocks from that river,
yet the sound of its rise and fall, its steady
on-going to the Columbia, to the Pacific,
doesn't loft into air and carry this far.

Cars coming across the narrow
lamp-lit bridge arcing its surface—
they lay down a schussh I catch.
Geese that fly from its edges
to neighborhood ponds and parks
wrinkle the air with their calls.
Raccoons making dens on its near bank
rustle in my garden at night. With eyes lit up
for garter snakes, they thresh flowers,
then tidy up, washing their hands
at the birdbath's edge.

A river's roam, that big sounding,
makes an under-rumble quieter yet—
an ocean-bound heartbeat
I press my ear earthward to hear.

## SLAKE

With the souls of my dead, I stand
by a river, breathing the underworld's
cool perfume. My mother, father,
Nana and Archie are near,
among others I can and cannot
name. Quiet lives here—just the slide
of water along an edge it's made
to touch. The only sound, a current
rubs against what waits.

Now geese, above. Their bleat
like air pushed through a reed—
hollow stalk begun in a meeting
of water and earth so it can
reach toward the sky. Then rowing,
close by—a boat borne along
by voiceless labor. An oar
plunged under, splashed up.
My wet feet taking root.

# FINISH

I rub my shoulder
against a doorframe's wood,
getting the feel of this creature
felled and transformed.
My fingers curve to knead blood
toward a muscle's hurt, lotion
into an elbow roughened by neglect.
Snubbing shoes, I let bare soles
reacquaint themselves
with the wear of pavement's grit.
Clothes serve the modest task
of long, soft friction.

Bit by bit, night by day,
I grow smoother-grained,
ready for light. Let me be
a mirror in which something else
might catch a glimpse of itself—
the burnished stone beneath
a lifetime of water, flowing.

## A LEGACY

I want to be this mouth
woven from twigs and string,
artifact of a neighborhood's fraying—
open, gaping at sky and rain.
I'll be last year's nest, what's left
on a limb so new to spring
it doesn't yet have leaves.
Old, but not closed: sure to be
used once more to kindle song,
or left to slump in the wind's tatter.

You be one of last year's fledglings,
now flying above. Look down
into this mouth you remember.
Nips of grass seed that once
moved through your body
took hold in the mud lining me.
Thin green tongues
speak up as you go by.

# II.
# WHAT YOU GATHER
# INTO YOURSELF

# DAWN

Outside, the air is colder
than you'd expect.
Breathe into your cupped hands.
Your breath is warm,
having rested a second or two
in your lungs—those twin chambers
flanking your heart as it works.

Open your hands. Send
your palms up to the sun.
Each outbound breath
is a small part of the sky
that lived in your body a while—
sky that cradled your core.

# WATER KNOWS ITS OWN KIND

A cloud reflected on the river
gathers more substance than it has
in the sky. On water's skin,
it's a white glare of exact shape.
In the sky, a blur of mist.

The sky is vast enough to be
nonchalant about what it carries.
Eager, the river takes
its cloud cousin onto itself,
giving the likeness buzz and tremble.

Only a fall to earth could break
this flattering portrait apart—
or a cloud-cloaked night,
when river and sky hold onto
darkness one-and-the-same.

## VANTAGE

Live where you can see
an ocean. Don't turn your back
to its blue. Let it seep in
through your sight.

A little salt in your blood,
your lymph, your sweat.
At the corner of each eye—
a tiny grain.

## BASIN

On a walk, your face catches
some of the rain—a bit
of river, mill pond, lake
coming around, slanted down.
Caught on your tongue,
raindrops taste sweet,
an ocean in its mild disguise.

What you gather into yourself
comes from as far away
as the whole world's girth,
from as close as what you
can reach. Your upturned hands
could cup to hold part of it—
carried with you: this earth's
steady recompense.

## SENSE

You can taste
only the part of rain falling
nearest your tongue.

Rain is that small,
that large—in pieces,
yet whole as a sky.

Sensing ozone,
cloud-scud, fog, and stream,
you hold in your mouth

rain's lowly beginnings,
its invisible rise—
that headlong fall.

Swallow,
and an ocean bathes
each of your cells.

## HALF EMPTY, HALF FULL

The glass is not an emptiness
it surrounds. The glass
does not create
what it may hold.

Spring is not paperwhites
rash in early bloom,
not the clear-night frost
bowing them to the ground.

Spring is that sweetness
beyond the word *wait.*
The glass is what—
when we drink—

our lips will touch.

## WHEN MEETING *the other*

Given arms, the sun
would choose to grow many.
Having many narrow arms,
the sun would—at each limb's end—
flare into a palm and fingers,
into the curves made for reaching.

Extremities of flame, of shine.
Hands that carry enough
heat and light to give away.

Be that sun. One small sun.

## LATE BLOOMING

Fall is the time for fire,
bonfire, bone fire,
limbs of another season
gathered to burn,
taken by heat,
        giving off heat.

And the leaf is finally
freed from that dazzle of green,
left to be
its own color,
        thin flame
given up to release—
    the longest
            burning of all.

## GATHER CLOSE

A brass apple sits atop
the book we laid down last spring
on a fireplace mantel. Wine-apples
wait outside in bared trees,
hiding within the spurs
coded for petals,
their sweet-fumed silk.

Winter. Time for what's
told only when light
makes itself scarce. Slight days,
cold-hefted nights lengthened
for listening. Wood smoke
curls and sidles, instructing us
in the ways of story.

Despite its gleam,
an apple of brass merely
decorates. The opened book—
a bud releasing pages one by one—
blooms white,
each read-aloud word
both fruit and sun.

# III.
# EVERYTHING HERE
# MUST TOUCH

## NARRATIVE DESCRIPTION, IMAGINATIVE LEAPS

The story begins as a figure, maybe
human, maybe not enough. A plain outline
filled in with key rings and dreams,
arrivals, departures, little nicks
in the process of healing, alarm clocks

set and ticking, a few too many scars.
Then the figure is carefully
cut out like a doll from paper,
taken away from everything else,
placed on another, blanker page.

What's left when the figure's gone
is more than a home minus
someone. What remains
is every possibility, each move
that figure didn't know enough to make.

What happens next becomes
much less a matter of conjecture
than bone for contention—
whole skeletons of malcontent,
no closet in sight.

## FOR SPECIAL EMPHASIS

Doesn't it figure that italics
were created to resemble
a sonneteer's written hand?
Those strokes and loops copied
from Petrarch—from his octaves, sestets,
iambs chumming in fives—first said
*pay attention,* or *read this as a quote.*

Now they say *title,* or *ship's name,*
or *what's too exotic—as yet—for English.*
This rendering of Petrarch's hand
leans forward to insist we see
*words as words, a work of art.*

## INK

Night in a bottle,
stars swimming
inside glass.

When we quit
dipping our pens,
when we emptied

darkness out of
its vessel,
did we stop

a constellation
from writing itself
onto a page?

## BREUGEL'S BABEL

The tower itself is a hive,
chambered with deep pockets
of peephole and door
from which the thick
viscous of gossip—that natter—
oozes like a honeyed tongue.

A cloud daubs itself between
the tower and whoever stands
in front of the painting
to look. Slice of diaphanous white.
Piece of drift placed there
by Breugel to keep
part of what aspires to heaven
away from our future eyes.

## ON SEEING SARGENT'S *CARNATION, LILY, LILY, ROSE*

Italian inks on sleek
high grade paper haven't prepared me
for the speechless fact that pieces
yes, of *light* lay themselves
on this surface in the very
way that flowed through
his blinked and unblinked
eyes, through arm, knuckles, fingertips,
the brush's shaft and bending
bristles. To adhere,

to *stay*. The miracle of not
flying away—pieces of light not finding
the neighborhood of color
so busy with traffic
they pick up and leave, sashay—
O Carnation, Lily, Lily's Echo,
Rose—not to sally, not to stray.

# CIRCUS

*—after Chagall*

Begin with a red fan
open in the bareback rider's hand.
I understand red. I know how it leaps
from her fingertips to the dress
pouring down the horse's grey side.
I see this fan and this dress,
how they ignore her pale breasts,
pretending to notice only her lips
and the flower sipping fire in her hair.

Red mouths the gossip
from her lips to the man's,
words that seem to disappear
into his shirt's dark sleeve
but are really caught in deep gathers
of her skirt. I know this fanfare,
trumpets starting a show
red began long ago.

# CHARLES BURCHFIELD,
# YOUR WORLD

Your hummingbird-moth at its flower
is beginning and end,
way to become indistinguishable—

milk of the morning's glory fused
into a needle beak.
Then gulps of your air

we've misnamed with the label *sky*
begin even before
your ground has begun.

Great ripples of leaf—green heat—
push up and away, their
milky secretions as wavered

as any earthly surface
of ridge, of rock can be—
star swimming in rivers of star.

## SLIP WORK

*—for the ceramicists*

Let one painted
leaf be bent
by your brush
over the lip
and onto the inner
rim of each bowl.
Let each bowl hold
at its depth
strokes of a painted
fruit so ripe and flushed
its color retains
summer's dust.

Let your black
be as fine and limber
as the three hairs
that tip your brush.
Each dark line, let it be
true to the sum
of flesh and grief,
shadow and sun.

# PAPER-CUTTING ART

His paper hide incised
with windows of whorl and rosette,
the cut-out ox lies down—
legs tucked under, head swung around
to look back at a crescent moon.
From his ornate backbone rises
a blooming vine that meets
the curve of moon
whose bottom prong shares an edge
with his chin tuft that touches—
*circle complete*—the vine.

To a single piece of paper,
someone in China plied scissors
the width of a thick pin,
cutting shapes out, air in.
Everything here must touch
something else, or end.

# IV.
# BROUGHT HERE
# FROM AFAR

## TRAVELER

Cast ashore
like some fleck of wood
brought here from afar
by the sea,

you reel—stunned
to breathe this reek of
strange urine, strange perfume
thick in saffron heat.

Here you are, foreign one,
familiar with only
the moon and stars,
a cloud-scraped sky,

the lidless eye of sun.
Take heart: only what floats
could be carried
as far as you've come.

## A CYCLADIC PROOF

Those who doubt
the ancient salt

of this sea
need only

watch their drying skin
glint, their limbs

turn to pale marble in
Agean sun.

# MOONRISE, ASTERIA

The Agean is gray, an even
undisturbed slate. The moon,
just a heartbeat away
from the water where it rose,

is the burnished red of some
huge unnatural jewel—
full, tumescently round,
heavy as it can bear to be.

What is the sky to such a moon?
What does a blood-gem care
for the airy dark spread out
beyond its rim?

Not an earthly thing.
It snubs the sky to pour itself,
in one long wavering gash,
across the salt gray sea.

## ON THE AGEAN

When every ship had sails, the sea
was a copse of pale trees
glinting sun from their leaves.
When all ships had sails, a harbor
was the wintery arbor—
thin trunks taking a leafless ease.

# NAVIGATION

Ships are painted white,
are made the bright of perfectly
round stones on a beach,
of seawater turned to salt by heat,
the blinding white of sand.

They're painted white so they can
sail away from a setting sun
toward a gray horizon. Then,
flashing the last of day's light,
they fall—in the one moment
you let them out of your sight—
off the earth's end.

## A MUNICIPAL SERVANT SERENADES AT THE PIER

Those who sing by the sea
draw a breeze
that lifts white wings
of foam from the deep.

When Evangelia sings—
sitting at the pier, her office hairdo
smoothed just so, breasts and belly
in a swimsuit's silky sling—

her voice is a riffle of doves
flown down from chalky cliffs,
it's the white and white
of wings above

saltwater's wimpled hue,
it's the poet's covey of words
streaming along
this blue, green, blue.

## SIREN

Away from the eye of a lighthouse,
                        waves—
            bilingual in the sun—
        send all telepathy
                    turning
    to braille of an ocean's floor.
                    Here the sound
                becomes a campaign
    of spume and spawn    of kelp
                    and shell,
        tumbleweed of the moon's pull.
            Here the sound is a
                brandished call,
            a baby's carriage
        lulled along,
                the torch song spun from
                sky to ground.

## ROOMS TO LET DREAM

So says a sign on a harbor hotel
of an island city named for Hermes.

So say the rooms behind numbered doors
hermetic against untimely waking.

From each door's quicksilver knob
hang the words *Do Not Disturb*—

magic posted to safely keep
those winged bouquets delivered in sleep.

# PHAETHON'S WARNING

To rest your head against the light
requires a cushion
part opaque, part translucent—
a mere half-light reaching you,
light halfway driven back.

Did you believe you could bear
such brilliance
whole, undeterred?
Even a god holds back
something. Even the sun keeps

its distance from earth.

# V.
# POLAR FLIGHT

Leaving Istanbul, I see
the Black Sea *isn't,*
is rather deep steely blue
flecked with white.
Shadows of clouds below us
ride its surface—watery black islands.
Strange that the sun
could be blocked by water vapor
gone busy and gregarious,
grown opaque, white.
Clouds seem too wispy for making
such dark, exacting copies.

What shadow does a berry
cast from inside a gull's belly,
what shade comes from
that hollow space inside
its buoyed bones?  What makes
the skimming, trembled
airplane shadow below?
I am—as much as anything else
inside this craft—
maker of a dark, cool twin.

After I'm sure I won't—
deep cloud cover minute after
minute beneath us—
I see Greenland
through a gap miles wide.
Not green land at all, it's dark, dun.
Water surrounding the land's rhizomes
is chock-a-block with ice chunks
achingly white. Fixing its cold
in an absence of color,
the ice throws green
back to the sun.

@

Flying west, as we refuse
to run out of daylight,
the young man beside me reads,
on and off, *A Brief History of Time.*
Page 31, diagram of some celestial body,
a vector drawn from it
to who knows what star—
the one who knows certainly not me,
this snooper over his shoulder.
The term *young man* itself quaint,
stiff to my ear. When did I begin
such a claim? I no longer
remember, and even *no longer* becomes
ephemeral, strange.

@

People walk up and down
the aisles as if adding to or subtracting from
500+ miles per hour were as easy
as one foot ahead of the other.
As if the wing I check each minute
through my poppet window were actually
pure silver instead of its flat
pedestrian gray.

⊛⊛

One layer of clouds moving
one way and another another,
or maybe one layer moving
with us, one against,
or maybe clouds in faster,
slower motion and us not—
*may* might simply be
another *is*.

⊛⊛

A movie star sans sound
repeats her smile from within the little
windows into her life
that hang from the cabin's ceiling.
Beautiful as ever, her lips
move in a pantomime I can
almost read—her words
sucked away by something approaching
the sound of speed.

⊛⊛

Over Nova Scotia—its offshore land
under water so clear
the ocean becomes just another
cloudless sky.

⊙⊙

Watching for the Statue of Liberty
I'm sure I won't spot,
in what must be a sound, I do sight
power boats and their wakes—
shower of tiny comets
held to slow motion.

⊙⊙

Near landing now. Our wing
tips down toward
a great winking and flashing
of metal roofs and car tops,
as we pass over suburbs, freeways,
and then I *see*. We are briefly
not a shadow,
but our self
a small, moving sun.

# About the Author

Paulann Petersen is a former Stegner Fellow at Stanford University whose poems have appeared in many publications including *Poetry, The New Republic, Prairie Schooner,* and *Wilderness Magazine.* She has three chapbooks (*Under the Sign of a Neon Wolf, The Animal Bride,* and *Fabrication*). Her first full-length collection of poems, *The Wild Awake,* was published by Confluence Press in 2002. A second, *Blood-Silk,* poems about Turkey, was published by Quiet Lion Press of Portland in 2004. Another, *A Bride of Narrow Escape* was published by Cloudbank Books as part of its Northwest Poetry Series in 2006 and was a finalist for the Oregon Book Award. Her work has been selected for *Poetry Daily* on the Internet, and for *Poetry in Motion,* which puts poems on busses and light rail cars in the Portland metropolitan area. In addition to having taught high school English (at West Linn High School, West Linn, Oregon, and at Mazama High School, Klamath Falls, Oregon), she's been on the faculty for the Creative Arts Community at Menucha, and has given workshops for Oregon Writers Workshop, Oregon State Poetry Association, Mountain Writers Series, OCTE and NCTE Conferences, and the Northwest Writing Institute at Lewis & Clark College. The recipient of the 2006 Literary Arts Stewart Holbrook Award for Outstanding Contributions to Oregon's Literary Life, she serves on the board for Friends of William Stafford, organizing the annual January William Stafford Birthday Events.

*Kindle* was designed by Herb Everett at Peace Rose Graphics in Eugene, Oregon. The cover was designed by Stephen Leflar of Portland. The book was printed on Accent Opaque 60# text using Bookman Old Style, and the cover was printed on 10 point C1S. *Kindle* was printed at Lithtex Printing in Hillsboro, Oregon.

A limited edition, letterpress chapbook of "Polar Flight" was published simultaneously with *Kindle*. It was designed by Stephen Leflar and Ed Rahyer and printed by Ed Rayher at Swamp Press in Massachusetts.